IT'S MY STATE!

KANSAS

David C. King

Richard Hantula

mc Marshall Cavendish
Benchmark

Published by Marshall Cavendish Benchmark
An imprint of Marshall Cavendish Corporation

Website: www.marshallcavendish.us

Other Marshall Cavendish Offices:
Marshall Cavendish International (Asia) Private Limited, 1 New Industrial Road, Singapore 536196 •
Marshall Cavendish International (Thailand) Co Ltd. 253 Asoke, 12th Flr, Sukhumvit 21 Road, Klongtoey Nua,
Wattana, Bangkok 10110, Thailand • Marshall Cavendish (Malaysia) Sdn Bhd, Times Subang, Lot 46, Subang
Hi-Tech Industrial Park, Batu Tiga, 40000 Shah Alam, Selangor Darul Ehsan, Malaysia

Marshall Cavendish is a trademark of Times Publishing Limited

Library of Congress Cataloging-in-Publication Data
King, David C.
      Kansas / David C. King, Richard Hantula. — 2nd ed.
         p. cm. — (It's my state!)
      Includes bibliographical references and index.
      Summary: "Surveys the history, geography, government, economy, and people of Kansas"—Provided by publisher.
      ISBN 978-1-60870-657-0 (print) — ISBN 978-1-60870-812-3 (ebook)
      1. Kansas—Juvenile literature. I. Hantula, Richard. II. Title.
   F681.3.K56 2013
   978.1—dc23   2011020732

Second Edition developed for Marshall Cavendish Benchmark by RJF Publishing LLC (www.RJFpublishing.com)
Series Designer, Second Edition: Tammy West/Westgraphix LLC

All maps, illustrations, and graphics © Marshall Cavendish Corporation. Maps and artwork on pages 6, 38, 39, 75, 76, and back cover by Christopher Santoro. Map and graphics on pages 10 and 46 by Westgraphix LLC.

The photographs in this book are used by permission and through the courtesy of:
Front cover: David Muenker/Alamy and Tom Dorsey/Associated Press (inset).
Alamy: Redmond Durrell, 5 (right); Clint Farlinger, 8; Andre Jenny, 9, 22, 74; Sara Blancett, 11; Dennie Cody, 12; Kevin Schafer, 13; North Wind Picture Archives, 19, 24; Buddy Mays, 21; Everett Collection Inc., 35, 37; Visions of America, LLC, 40; Ninette Maumus, 47; World History Archive, 48 (left); Pictorial Press Ltd., 49; Stock Connection Blue, 50; Michael Snell, 53; Ilene MacDonald, 54; Danita Delimont, 58, 66; Grant Heilman Photography, 62; AGStockUSA, 64; David R. Frazier/Photolibrary Inc., 67; Phil Degginger, 71 (left); Transtock Inc., 73.
Associated Press: Associated Press, 14, 15, 20 (left), 44, 48 (right), 51, 52. **Getty Images:** Time & Life Pictures, 41; Getty Images, 42.
The Granger Collection, New York: 27. **Kansas State Historical Society:** 60. **North Wind Picture Archives:** 25, 28, 30, 31, 33.
Superstock: Stock Connection, 4; Minden Pictures, 5 (left), 16; Design Pics, 17; NHPA, 20 (right); Elena Elisseeva/Superfusion, 65; George Ostertag, 70; Belinda Images, 71 (right).

Printed in Malaysia (T).
135642

CONTENTS

THE SUNFLOWER STATE

State Flower: Sunflower

The sunflower is a familiar sight throughout Kansas. It generally ranges in height from 3 to 15 feet (1 to 5 meters). The center, or disk, of its flower can be brown, orange, or purple. Sunflower seeds are valuable food sources. Oil from the seeds is used in cooking and to make margarine, as well as to make the type of diesel fuel called biodiesel. The petals are used to make a bright yellow dye.

State Tree: Eastern Cottonwood

For pioneers heading west on the Oregon Trail or the Santa Fe Trail, the eastern cottonwood trees of what is now Kansas were a welcome sight. Trees for firewood or for shade were scarce on the prairie, but the cottonwoods flourished along the banks of rivers and streams.

State Bird: Western Meadowlark

The western meadowlark is easily identified by its intricate, flutelike song. Meadowlarks' nests are simple grass mounds built on the ground. A meadowlark's favorite foods are insects and seeds.

State Animal: American Bison

The area that is now Kansas was once open prairie land where enormous herds of American bison (sometimes also called buffalo) roamed. By 1900, bison had nearly all been killed in Kansas, but the efforts of ranchers, conservationists, and others have helped the animals make a strong comeback. Small herds can now be seen in several Kansas wildlife reserves and parks.

State Insect: Honeybee

Honeybees play an important part in the Kansas economy. They help pollinate many of the state's crops, and they also produce valuable honey and beeswax.

State Reptile: Ornate Box Turtle

The word ornate means decorative or attractive, and this box turtle gets its name from the yellow markings on its shell. These reptiles eat insects, worms, spiders, grass, and berries. They are active in the spring, summer, and fall but hide below the ground to hibernate during the winter months.

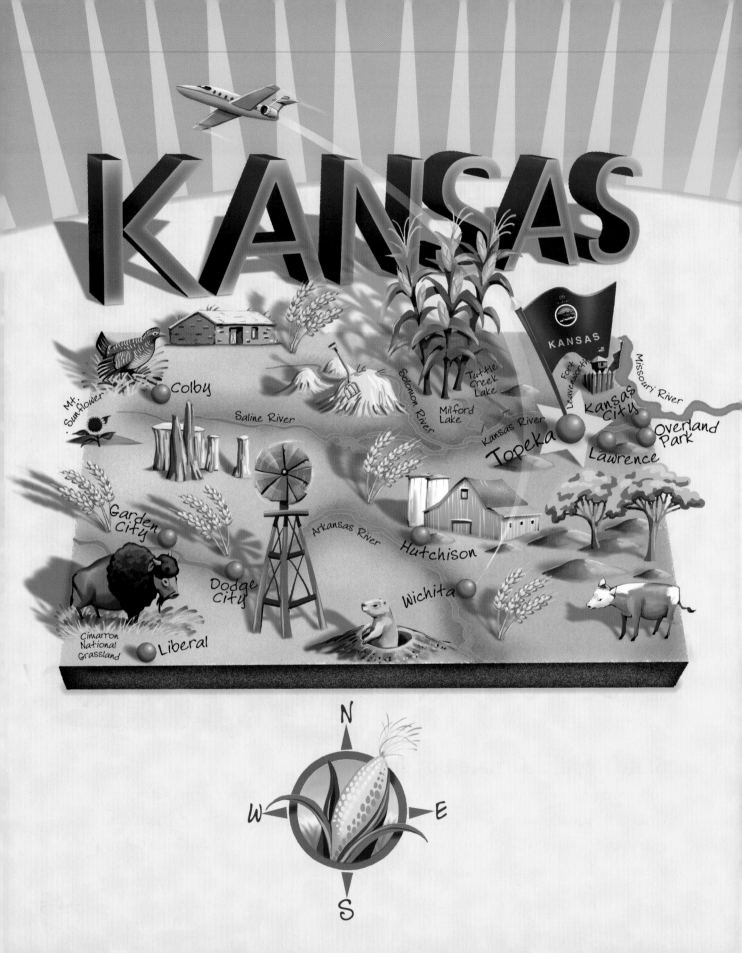

1

The Sunflower State

When Americans think of Kansas, they may have many different pictures in their minds. Some might have images of its colorful past, including huge herds of bison thundering across the prairie, a pioneer wagon train heading west on the Oregon Trail, or cowboys riding into a Wild West town like Abilene or Dodge City. Others might think of modern Kansas, perhaps images of endless fields of wheat ripening in the sun, a sleek new single-engine jet rolling out of a factory in Wichita, or crowds cheering a football showdown between the University of Kansas Jayhawks and the Wildcats of Kansas State University. Kansas is all these things and more.

It is one of the bigger U.S. states. It has a land area of 81,762 square miles (211,764 square kilometers), giving it a rank of thirteenth among the fifty states. Kansas is divided into 105 counties, making it one of the few states with more than a hundred counties. In population, Kansas ranks thirty-third among the states.

Kansas lies within two large geographic regions: the Central Lowlands and the Great Plains. The Central Lowlands cover the eastern third of the state. The western two-thirds of the state are part of the Great Plains.

Quick Facts

KANSAS BORDERS

North	Nebraska
South	Oklahoma
East	Missouri
West	Colorado

Hundreds of varieties of wildflowers bloom in the Flint Hills region.

The Central Lowlands

If you fly over Kansas or travel across it by car or train, the land may seem flat and uninteresting. When you look more closely, however, parts of the state offer scenes of spectacular geographic variety. The landscape of the northeast was largely shaped by glaciers—slow-moving sheets of ice. During the past 2 million years or so, such ice sheets at times covered much of North America. Roughly 600,000 to 700,000 years ago, the ice crept across what is now the northeastern part of Kansas, reaching as far south as the Kansas River. As the glaciers moved, they carved up the land, creating hills and valleys. The glaciers' movements also left large deposits of nutrient-rich soil in the region. Because of this fertile land, this part of the state is ideal for farming. The northeastern section of Kansas is also the most heavily wooded part of the state.

The Kansas River runs through the Central Lowlands. South of the Kansas River, most of the Central Lowlands consist of gently rolling hills. The Flint Hills are located in this area. Along with flint, they consist of limestone and shale that formed more than 250 million years ago. Some of the hills are as high as 400 feet (120 m). From those heights, there are beautiful views of the valleys below. Tall grasses such as bluestem grass grow in those areas. Sometimes this part of the state is called the Bluestem Region. It is the only place in the United States where

More than 600,000 people live in the city of Wichita and the suburbs around it.

you can still find a few areas of true, never-plowed prairie. One such location is the Tallgrass Prairie National Preserve in Chase County.

East of the Flint Hills is a region of long ridges, or escarpments, that have a steep, east-facing slope on one side and a gentle slope on the other. This type of feature is called a cuesta, and the region is known as the Osage cuestas. The cuestas are made of limestone and shale that formed some 300 million years ago. The escarpments are up to 200 feet (60 m) high.

The Central Lowlands are home to Kansas's largest cities. Kansas City, Overland Park, and Olathe are near the state's northeastern border with Missouri. Moving westward from those cities, you will find Topeka, the state's capital. Wichita, Kansas's most populous city, is located in the south-central part of the Central Lowlands, along the Arkansas River.

The Great Plains

The Great Plains region, which covers the central and western two-thirds of Kansas, is the flattest part of the state. The land slopes gently upward from about 700 feet (213 m) above sea level in the east to more than 4,000 feet (1,200 m) at the Colorado border in the west. The Smoky Hills are in north-central Kansas. In the south, sand hills, or dunes, can be found in some places

Kansas Counties

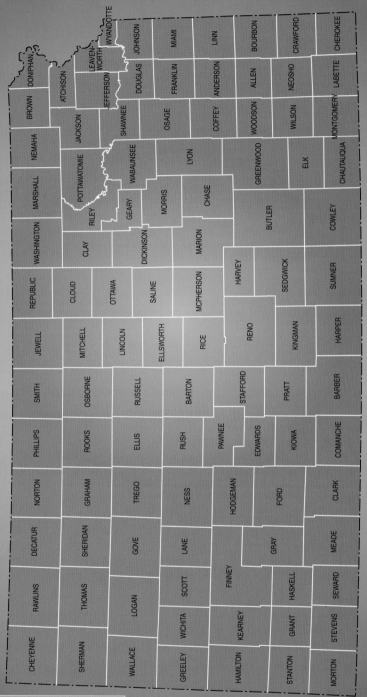

Kansas has 105 counties.

in the lowlands along the Arkansas River. Prairie land covers large parts of the Great Plains in Kansas.

Several million years ago, streams and winds moved enormous amounts of sand, gravel, and other material from the Rocky Mountains eastward, forming huge deposits in what is now the Great Plains. These deposits became natural storage tanks—called aquifers—for underground water. The water in these aquifers makes extensive irrigation possible. The aquifers are also important sources of drinking water. The largest aquifer in the Great Plains is the Ogallala Aquifer, which extends from southern South Dakota through western Kansas to northern Texas. It contains an enormous amount of water. The water, however, is being pumped out faster than it can be replaced by rainwater and water from melting snow. If the aquifer continues to lose water, farming in the area will become more difficult.

Erosion has played a major role in shaping the geographic features of the Great Plains area of Kansas. Erosion is the gradual wearing away of land by wind and water. For example, the grasslands of the plains are crisscrossed by shallow gullies, which are also called draws. The gullies were carved out over thousands of years.

Quick Facts

HIGHEST AND LOWEST

The highest point in Kansas is at a spot called Mount Sunflower in Wallace County at the western end of the state. It is 4,039 feet (1,231 m) above sea level. The lowest point in the state, at 679 feet (207 m), is on the Verdigris River in Montgomery County in the southeast.

The Castle Rock limestone formation is located on private property, but visitors to the site are welcome.

At times over the past few hundred million years, the land that includes present-day Kansas was the floor of a sea. Years of geological change altered the landscape. When the waters dried, limestone-rich land was left behind. Erosion of the deposits of limestone and chalk (a form of soft limestone) in western Kansas created some of the most spectacular land features in the state. One example is Castle Rock in Gove County, in the Smoky Hills. It is made up of chalk pillars that rise above the grassland like the towers of a castle. Several miles to the west is the site known as Monument Rocks. This site's amazing natural structures, which reach as high as 70 feet (21 m), are often called chalk pyramids.

Because the area that is now Kansas was underwater millions of years ago, fossil hunters and scientists today find the remains of many prehistoric sea creatures. The fossilized remains of these ancient animals are embedded within the many layers of rock in western

In Their Own Words

A great many people find it dull and monotonous. . . . But when I [reach] the open plains, something happens. I'm home. I can breathe.

—American novelist Willa Cather (1873–1947), writing about the prairie

Kansas. Fossils found in Kansas are displayed in museums around the world.

Rivers and Lakes

There are two major river systems in Kansas. The Kansas River (also known as the Kaw River) drains the northern part of the state. Its tributaries include the Big Blue and the Republican rivers. At Kansas City, it flows into the Missouri River, which forms the border of the state's northeast corner. The other major system is the Arkansas River. It comes into the state from Colorado, flows through the southern part of the state, and continues through Oklahoma and Arkansas to the Mississippi River. The Smoky Hill River is another long river that begins in Colorado. It stretches across more than half of Kansas.

Fossil remains of the sea creatures called crinoids have been found in the limestone of western Kansas.

Kansas has more than 200 lakes. Most of these lakes are human-made. In the southeast, for example, the strip-mining of coal created deep depressions in the ground. The topsoil was stripped away in order to reach the coal. Surface water and underground water gradually filled the depressions, creating sparkling lakes.

The largest lakes were created after disastrous droughts in the 1930s. The federal government had engineers build dams on several rivers, forming these lakes. Milford Lake on the Republican River is the state's largest lake and covers

Completed in the 1960s, Milford Lake is popular with boaters and fishers.

16,000 acres (6,500 hectares). Tuttle Creek Lake, covering 12,500 acres (5,100 ha), is Kansas's second-largest lake. Milford, Tuttle Creek, and other large lakes provide flood control, irrigation, and drinking water for cities and towns. Lakes of all sizes are also used for fishing, boating, and other forms of recreation.

Climate

Kansas has a continental climate. This is a climate that is usually found in the middle of a continent. One of the main features of a continental climate is very cold winters and hot summers. Kansas's flat land allows cold air to blow in from the north during winter. In January, temperatures average about 30 degrees Fahrenheit (−1 degree Celsius). The state's coldest temperature was recorded in Lebanon in February 1905. It was −40 °F (−40 °C). During the summer months, hot winds and fierce thunderstorms sweep north from the Gulf of Mexico. The temperature in Kansas in July is around 78 °F (26 °C). The hottest

Quick Facts

WINDY CITY
Dodge City, in southern Kansas, has average winds blowing at almost 14 miles (22 kilometers) per hour. Some say that this makes it the windiest city in the United States outside Alaska.

Western Kansas is in the part of the central United States called Tornado Alley. Tornadoes occur more often in this region than anywhere else in the country.

recorded temperature in the state was 121 °F (49 °C) at both Fredonia and Alton in July 1936.

Kansas weather can change quickly and oftentimes unexpectedly. Kansans are familiar with thunderstorms, tornadoes, hail, and even winter blizzards. Precipitation— rain, snow, and other kinds of moisture—falls in uneven amounts across the state. Southeastern Kansas receives about 40 inches (100 centimeters) or more each year. This amount of precipitation is good for farming. But the precipitation level declines steadily from the eastern to western parts of Kansas. The western region, near the border of Colorado, receives only 16 to 18 inches (40 to 45 cm) each year.

Kansas Wildlife

Large areas of the state are treeless, but several million trees have been planted since the 1930s. This was done to hold the soil in place and to serve as windbreaks. Hilly areas have a large variety of trees, including ash, elm, maple, and oak. Cottonwoods are common along rivers and streams.

The grasslands are naturally treeless. In the past, the grazing of wild bison and the burning of natural wildfires prevented scrub forests (forests consisting

American Indians began using sunflower seeds as a food source thousands of years ago.

mostly of shrubs and grasses) from taking over the land. Today, however, the grasslands are maintained by managed herds of cattle or bison. Controlled burns started by humans also help rid the area of scrub.

The list of Kansas wildflowers is topped by the state flower—the sunflower—which blooms from mid-summer to late fall in all parts

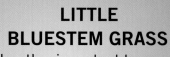

Quick Facts

LITTLE BLUESTEM GRASS
Unlike other important types of grasses native to Kansas, the type of bluestem grass called little bluestem is found throughout the state. In 2010 it was named the official state grass.

STATE AMPHIBIAN

Kansas named the barred tiger salamander its official state amphibian in 1994. These animals live throughout the state. But finding them can be hard. In the summer and winter they tend to stay in moist places (such as other animals' burrows) where their skin won't get dry, and they come out only at night. In spring and fall, however, they are more active. Barred tiger salamanders can live for up to twenty years and may grow as long as 14 inches (36 cm), making them among the world's biggest land-living salamanders.

of the state. Aster, clover, columbine, daisies, thistles, verbena, and morning glories give the prairie lands splashes of color for most of the year.

Different types of animals live in Kansas. Mammals such as coyotes, opossums, jackrabbits, prairie dogs, raccoons, muskrats, and squirrels are common throughout the state.

Birds are also plentiful in the skies, trees, or prairie grasses. Some types include robins, meadowlarks, blue jays, crows, and cardinals. Several varieties of hawk nest in Kansas and can be seen soaring across the blue skies.

The rivers, streams, and lakes in Kansas attract waterfowl. These include ducks, geese, and swans. In the waters, fish such as bass, bluegills, trout, and catfish swim and breed. Fish such as crappie, sunfish, sauger, and walleye are often stocked in—or added to—the state's waterways. These fish play an important part in the ecosystem. At the same time, they provide sport for people who enjoy fishing.

The state's deer and pronghorns are now more numerous than they were a hundred years ago. Before the 1900s, large populations of these animals roamed freely across the state. Loss of habitat and overhunting decreased their numbers. But with humans paying more attention to protecting these animal populations, their numbers are growing.

Animals in Danger

The bison are an example of an animal population brought back from the brink of extinction. In other words, they were on the verge of completely dying out. When pioneers first crossed the Great Plains in the early 1800s, they encountered huge herds of bison. There were 60 million or more of these big, shaggy beasts in North America. The Indians of the Great Plains had hunted the bison for centuries. They depended on the animals for food, clothing, shelter, tools, and weapons. But they killed only what they needed, used most of the animal, and did not threaten the herds' continued existence.

The arrival of settlers from the East and from Europe caused the bison population to decrease. Bison were hunted for their hides, and settlers fenced off lands where bison used to roam. When railroads were built across the Great Plains, the railroad companies hired professional hunters to shoot bison for meat to feed the thousands of railroad workers. They also let passengers shoot the animals from trains for sport. Bison were also hunted to hurt the Indians of the Great Plains. The reduction in this important food source helped force Indian groups to surrender and move onto reservations. Some historians and scientists believe that, along with human interference, droughts during the 1800s also hurt bison populations. By 1900, only a few hundred bison remained. Through

In the 1800s, millions of bison were shot by hunters. Sometimes the meat and hides were used. At other times, animals were left to rot where they fell.

breeding programs and protective laws, the bison population in the United States has slowly grown. Bison will never be able to roam across the Kansas plains as they did hundreds of years ago. But today there are some 200,000 bison living in herds on private ranches and on government land throughout the country, including in Kansas.

Kansans are mindful of the state's wildlife and have made efforts to protect their native plants and animals.

Plants & Animals

Bluestem Grass

Pioneers heading west sometimes found that dense prairie grass in eastern Kansas made wagon travel difficult. This prairie grass is called bluestem grass. The type called big bluestem can reach 6 feet (1.8 m) or more in height. Big bluestem is also called "turkey foot," because of the forked shape of the flower stem. Settlers found that bluestem grass was good for grazing cattle.

Copperhead

The two most common kinds of poisonous snakes in Kansas are rattlesnakes and copperheads. Copperheads, which can grow to a length of about 3 feet (1 m), get their name from the reddish-brown color of their heads. These snakes are helpful to farmers and ranchers—and to the ecosystem—because they control the rodent population.

Prairie Chicken

The prairie chicken, a type of grouse, is a popular game bird, which means that it is favored by hunters. The bird's brown feathers and rounded dark tail help it blend in with prairie plants. Prairie chickens are found in several plains states. There are two different kinds in Kansas: the greater prairie chicken and the lesser prairie chicken. Kansas and Nebraska have the largest populations of greater prairie chickens. Kansas has the largest population of lesser prairie chickens.

Catfish

The waters of Kansas are often stocked with catfish, and the fish populations seem to be thriving. These fish are popular among sport fishers. They are found nearly everywhere in the state.

Pronghorn

Like bison and deer, pronghorns were overhunted and nearly became extinct. Over the past thirty years, the efforts of farmers, hunters, and conservationists have helped their population increase. Today, there are roughly 2,000 in western Kansas, and many more live in other states. A pronghorn (sometimes also called an antelope) stands about 30 to 40 inches (75 to 100 cm) high at the shoulder. It is graceful, fast, and nimble. Over long distances, it is the world's fastest land mammal. It can go up to 60 miles (100 km) per hour and can keep up a speed of 30 miles (50 km) per hour for miles.

Black-Tailed Prairie Dog

Black-tailed prairie dogs have short tails tipped with black. They live in connected tunnels underneath the soil of the Great Plains, including western Kansas. Many farmers consider prairie dogs pests, and as a result, the black-tailed prairie dog population has greatly decreased. However, conservation efforts by concerned residents continue to help these small mammals.

From the Beginning

The people of Kansas have many reminders of the state's colorful, and often exciting, history. Restored forts recall the days when the U.S. Cavalry protected wagon trains heading west. In towns such as Dodge City, historic sections have been restored to look as they did when cowboys drove herds of cattle to the railroads. County fairs remind people of other episodes in the state's history. Annual festivals celebrate the history and culture of different groups that made Kansas their home through the years.

The First Residents

The story of humans in the area now known as Kansas begins with the people whom historians call Paleo-Indians ("Ancient Indians"). These people are thought to have lived in the region as early as 11,000 to 12,000 years ago. They had a nomadic lifestyle, with no fixed home. For food, they hunted large animals and gathered berries, seeds, and plant roots, as well as creatures such as clams.

The climate gradually changed, becoming warmer, and many large animals became scarce or even extinct. During what is called the Archaic period, which began about 7000 BCE and lasted

Quick Facts

STATE NAME
Kansas is named after the Kansa Indians, who were also known as the Kaw Indians.

Historic Front Street re-creates the look of Dodge City when it was an Old West cow town in the 1870s and 1880s.

Plains Indians used both horses and dogs to help them move their possessions as they followed bison herds.

for several thousand years, many people adopted a somewhat more settled, less nomadic, lifestyle. Plants and small animals came to make up a larger part of their food.

The Archaic period was followed by the Woodland period, which lasted roughly until about 1000 CE. Woodland people were known for using pottery and, increasingly, the bow and arrow. While continuing to get food by hunting and gathering, they also began planting crops such as corn. Some built burial mounds for their dead.

During the centuries after the Woodland period, bison hunting became an increasingly important part of Indian life in the region that is now Kansas. When Indians killed a bison, they made use of nearly the entire animal. The fur and hide were made into clothing, tepees, and shields. Tools and weapons were created from the bison's horns and bones. Much of the meat was dried and cut into strips called pemmican. This dried meat remained edible for a long time. The raising of crops such as corn, squash, and beans also became more and more important. Settlements tended to be bigger and more permanent.

Horses, brought to North America by the Spanish in the 1500s, created a revolution in the lives of many of the Indians of the Great Plains. The Comanche and others became expert riders. The horses helped them to follow bison herds as the animals grazed and migrated. The introduction of horses also made tepees more popular. Tepees were made of animal hide and long wooden poles and were ideal for groups who followed herds for food. The tepees were easy to put together and take apart, and horses were used to transport the long poles. By the time Europeans began establishing outposts in the area that is now Kansas, several different Indian groups lived in the region. They included the Kansa, Osage, Pawnee, and Wichita.

The Europeans

The first Europeans to reach the Great Plains were Spanish explorers and missionaries led by Francisco Vásquez de Coronado. Coronado was searching for mythical cities of gold. Beginning in an area that is now Mexico but was then held by Spain, he headed north. By 1541, he reached as far as present-day Kansas, but he never found the golden cities. The missionaries came to the region looking to spread the Catholic faith. Another major Spanish expedition, headed by Juan de Oñate, reached the region in 1601.

In 1682, the French explorer René-Robert Cavelier, sieur de La Salle, claimed for France all the land whose rivers flowed into the Mississippi River. This included the region that is now Kansas. In the early 1700s, French fur traders and explorers from France's colony of Canada set up outposts in the region. The first long-lasting European settlement in what is now Kansas was Fort de Cavagnial, established in 1744 by the French on the west bank of the Missouri River near today's Leavenworth. It existed for some twenty years.

The Spanish explorer Francisco de Coronado covered a distance of well over 1,000 miles (1,600 kilometers) on the expedition that took him from Mexico to what is now Kansas.

The region that includes present-day Kansas became a part of the United States in 1803. This was a result of the Louisiana Purchase. According to this agreement, the United States bought a huge area of land from France called the Louisiana Territory. This vast territory, stretching westward from the Mississippi River, doubled the size of the United States. It gave Americans an enormous western frontier to explore and settle. In 1804, an expedition led by Meriwether Lewis and William Clark headed up the Missouri River. It even went beyond the Louisiana Purchase, crossing the Rocky Mountains and reaching the Pacific Ocean before returning in 1806. An expedition led by Zebulon Pike headed west across present-day Kansas in 1806. Pike reached the Rockies and then turned southward, eventually entering Spanish territory. Such expeditions gave Americans their first detailed information about their new western lands.

Settling the Land

In the early 1800s, the United States was growing rapidly, and more and more settlers were moving into the region east of the Mississippi River. This created problems for the Indian groups living there. For the most part, the new settlers thought that the region's land should be used for farming. Many felt that the Indians' use of the land mostly as hunting grounds was wasting useful resources. The Indians were unhappy with the arrival of the new people who claimed the land and took away their native homelands and hunting grounds. Warfare between settlers and Indians broke out. The federal government eventually moved many of the Indians in the region onto land west of the Mississippi River. This area was designated as Indian Territory.

Present-day Kansas was part of this territory. Between roughly 1830 and 1845, a number of American Indian groups were moved into the Kansas area, near today's border between Kansas and Missouri. Among them were the Ojibwe (also called Chippewa), Lenape (or Delaware), Fox, Iowa, Shawnee, Kickapoo, Wyandot (or Huron), and Potawatomi Indians. Life on this new land was difficult for these Indians. The landscape east of the Mississippi River was much different from the land in the west. The Indians had to adapt to new lifestyles.

A group of Kansa Indians met with U.S. government officials in Washington, D.C., in 1857 to protest the loss of their land to white settlers.

However, this resettlement of the Indians did not last long. Land-hungry white settlers from farther east were already pushing across the Mississippi River and into Indian Territory. Many settlers from the Ohio River valley moved into northern and eastern Kansas. Farms and settlements were established across the region. Missions were also built in the area.

In 1821, a trader named William Becknell opened a wagon-train trail that began at the Missouri River, crossed what is now Kansas, and proceeded on to Santa Fe, New Mexico, covering a total distance of about 1,200 miles (1,900 km). This trail was called the Santa Fe Trail. To help protect the trail, Colonel Henry Leavenworth of the U.S. Army in 1827 established a military outpost not far from the site where Fort de Cavagnial had stood. The U.S. outpost was called Cantonment Leavenworth. Its name later became Fort Leavenworth. It is still in operation today.

The Santa Fe Trail was eventually joined by the Oregon Trail. Pioneers traveling along the Oregon Trail crossed through the northeastern part of present-day Kansas on their way to what was then known as the Oregon Country in the Pacific Northwest. Between 1840 and 1870, an estimated 300,000

Pioneers crossing the country on the Oregon Trail packed their belongings into large covered wagons sometimes known as prairie schooners.

pioneers traveled the more than 2,000 miles (3,200 km) of the Oregon Trail. The trail went through the sites of Topeka, Lawrence, and several other present-day Kansas towns.

By the 1850s the U.S. government relocated the Indians to make room for new settlement. Some Indian leaders were told to move onto reservations—small areas of land set aside for a few tribes—but most were told to move their people onto land that includes present-day Oklahoma. The area that is now Kansas would no longer be a part of Indian Territory and would be open to settlers. Many Indians felt betrayed by the government. They moved their people onto the Great Plains and joined the Plains groups in waging war against settlers and against the U.S. government. The fighting in Kansas did not end until 1878.

In the 1850s, some members of Congress had another reason for wanting the Indians removed from Kansas. They were planning to build the nation's first transcontinental railroad. This railroad would cross the continent, connecting the West Coast with the existing railroad network in the eastern part of the country. The route eventually chosen for the first intercontinental railroad went through Nebraska rather than Kansas. However, railroad lines were also built in Kansas connecting with points to the north, west, and south.

FROM WYANDOTT TO KANSAS CITY

In the 1840s the Wyandot Indians were forced to move from Ohio to Indian Territory in Kansas. They purchased land from the Lenape Indians and built a community they named Wyandot (or Wyandott). White settlers began moving into the area in the following decade. Along with whites, Indians continued to play important roles in the community. In 1859 the town became the center, or county seat, of a newly organized county called Wyandott. Railroad construction and an influx of European immigrants helped the city of Wyandotte (as the name came to be spelled) grow fast. Nearby, a town called Kansas City began to take shape at the end of the 1860s. In 1886, Wyandotte and the two smaller towns of Kansas City and Armourdale were combined into one city, which received the name Kansas City.

Slavery and Civil War

By the 1850s, Kansas found itself in the center of a growing conflict over slavery in the United States. Slavery was one of the main issues that led to the start of the Civil War in 1861. During the 1850s, most people in the Northern states insisted that slavery must not be allowed in the new territories and states in the West. Southerners did not agree. Congress decided to let the voters in each new territory decide whether or not to permit slavery. This solution was called popular sovereignty, and it was written into the Kansas-Nebraska Act of 1854, which established the Kansas and Nebraska territories. The Kansas Territory reached as far west as the Rocky Mountains. Hundreds of pioneer families— many sponsored by New England antislavery societies—moved to Kansas. They hoped to establish a territorial government that would not allow slavery. But they were opposed by slavery supporters who crossed over from Missouri, some entering Kansas only long enough to vote.

The conflict between supporters and opponents of slavery lasted for several years. There were frequent outbreaks of violence that claimed dozens of lives and led people to call the territory Bleeding Kansas. In an incident in 1856, a group of armed supporters of slavery from Missouri, called Border Ruffians,

attacked the town of Lawrence, which was a center of opposition to slavery. They destroyed newspaper offices and burned down a hotel. This angered a man named John Brown, who was a fierce enemy of slavery. Brown immediately led a raid on suspected slavery supporters living near Pottawatomie Creek, killing five of them. Three years later, Brown led a larger raid on Harpers Ferry, Virginia, hoping to start a nationwide revolution by slaves. The raid collapsed, and Brown was arrested, found guilty of treason, and executed.

The slavery issue hampered the Kansas Territory's efforts to gain admission to the Union as a state. Three different constitutions were prepared, including one that permitted slavery. None of them was accepted by Congress. Kansans tried again. They wrote a fourth constitution, which did not allow slavery. It won approval by Kansas's voters in 1859. In January 1861, Congress finally agreed to grant statehood to Kansas. President James Buchanan signed the measure into law on January 29, 1861. The new state included only the eastern portion of the original Kansas Territory. The western portion became part of a new territory called Colorado.

Less than three months after Kansas gained statehood, the nation was split apart by the Civil War. More than 20,000 Kansans fought in the war. In late 1864, one of the largest cavalry battles of the Civil War was fought in Kansas at Mine Creek near the Missouri border. Confederate General Sterling Price had been attempting to strike at Union forces through Missouri. Price's men, who numbered about 8,000, were attacked by some 2,800 Union troops. Even though the Confederates had a numerical superiority, they were soundly defeated by the Union forces.

After the war ended in 1865, thousands of veterans moved to Kansas to start new lives. Many of them, along with other new settlers, benefited from the Homestead Act, which Congress had passed in 1862. This law allowed a family to own a farmstead of 160 acres (65 ha) simply by living on and working the land for a period of five years.

The Cowboy Era

Kansas experienced another great change beginning in the late 1860s. As railroad construction inched across Kansas, cattle ranchers in Texas began to drive large herds of cattle north to meet the railroad. These cattle drives were long and dangerous, but they were the most efficient way to get the long-horned steers to

Millions of cattle were driven north on the Chisholm Trail from Texas to railroad depots in Kansas.

markets in the fast-growing cities of the East. The result was the era of cowboys, cattle drives, and "Wild West" towns.

Abilene was the first of the major frontier cattle towns, although Dodge City became the most famous. Other cattle towns were Ellsworth, Newton, and Wichita. After long, hard weeks on the trail, the cowboys rode into town eager to "bust loose" in saloons and gambling halls. Magazines, newspapers, "dime novels," and other media (even modern-day movies) have often exaggerated when describing the rowdiness of the Wild West. There was lawlessness, but there were relatively few shoot-outs in the streets. For the most part, business owners and other people trying to establish the area did not want their towns to be thought of as lawless. They wanted the area to appear peaceful, thereby attracting more business.

Quick Facts

JAYHAWK STATE

Kansas is known as the Jayhawk State, but no one is exactly sure where the term comes from. One story is that it comes from a legendary bird from Ireland called the jayhawk. Unfortunately, no one knows what this bird was supposed to look like. Some of the fighters in the period of Bleeding Kansas, especially those opposed to slavery, were called Jayhawkers, as was a regiment of Kansas's volunteers during the Civil War. Today, the sports teams of the University of Kansas are nicknamed Jayhawks.

The lively days of the cattle drives lasted only about twenty years. The trails became more and more difficult to travel because farmers and ranchers began fencing in their lands with a new invention called barbed wire. At the same time, more railroads were built in Texas, reducing the need for ranchers to drive their herds north to Kansas to reach railroad junctions. Also, in early 1886, Kansas was hit by the worst blizzard in its history. Tens of thousands of cattle were killed. In some areas, 80 percent of the cattle on the open range were lost. The following year, a period of drought began. By 1890, the long drives were over, and cowboys were working on fenced-in ranches.

Thousands of workers from all over the United States and from many other countries helped build railroads across the American West in the second half of the 1800s.

The Railroads

The growth of the railroads in the 1800s changed the face of Kansas. Towns across the state were eager to have a railroad nearby. As more track was built, they competed to be along the railway line. The railroads provided business in the form of livestock, supplies, and travelers. Towns that were along the railroads' paths tended to flourish, while others lost business, in some cases turning into ghost towns.

The Atchison, Topeka, and Santa Fe Railway was one of the railroads that played a large part in developing Kansas's towns and cities. Parts of the Atchison, Topeka, and Santa Fe followed the same route as the Santa Fe Trail. Branches of the railroad helped cattle towns such as Wichita and Dodge City become even busier business centers. The Atchison, Topeka, and Santa Fe continued to operate until 1995, when it joined with the Burlington Northern Railroad to create the huge Burlington Northern and Santa Fe Railway, today known as the BNSF.

Besides bringing in business, the growth of railroads in Kansas—as well as in other states—helped the population increase. As more of Kansas became easily accessible, more people decided to live in the state. Workers found employment

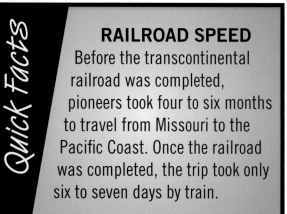
laying tracks and doing other jobs for the railroad. The work was hard and dangerous, and it did not always pay well, but many were happy to at least have jobs. The railroads also brought new faces to the state. Many of the state's first Mexican and Mexican-American settlers from the west came to the region by train.

America's Breadbasket

In the 1870s and 1880s, thousands of European immigrants settled in the new territories and states of the Great Plains. They were lured by the advertising of the railroad companies. Railroad companies had been given more than 10 million acres (4 million ha) of Kansas land. They sold much of it to immigrants from Europe. The railroad companies competed vigorously for the settlers because the companies' income would come from shipping farm goods east and bringing manufactured goods west.

The Civil War had ended slavery in America, but many freed slaves found themselves cast adrift in an unfriendly world. Most were uneducated and had few job skills. In addition, many whites in the North and the South continued to harbor deep prejudices against African Americans. In the late 1870s, several church groups and other organizations encouraged freed slaves to establish homesteads in Kansas. The idea caught on, and thousands of blacks joined the movement. This migration became known as the Black Exodus, and those who took part were called Exodusters.

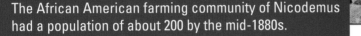

The African American farming community of Nicodemus had a population of about 200 by the mid-1880s.

Many African Americans, however, found it hard to establish homes and farms in Kansas. The cost of setting up a farm was high, and most of the freed slaves did not have enough money. Some ended up working on other people's farms or left the region entirely. In 1877, the town of Nicodemus was founded, populated mostly by freed slaves from Kentucky. They withstood the hardships and established a strong community. Nicodemus was not along any major railroads, and over the years the population decreased. Nicodemus still remains today. It was designated a national historic landmark district in 1976, and a national historic site twenty years later.

In the late 1800s, new tools and techniques opened up the prairie lands to farming. New steel plows could easily slice through the thick sod. In addition, immigrants from Russia brought a new form of winter wheat

In Their Own Words

When I landed on the soil, I looked on the ground and I says this is free ground. Then I looked on the heavens, and I says them is free and beautiful heavens. Then I looked within my heart, and I says to myself I wonder why I never was free before?

—Exoduster John Solomon Lewis, on his arrival in Kansas

called Turkey Red. Planted in the fall, winter wheat ripens by early summer, so farmers could avoid problems such as the droughts and insects of midsummer.

By the 1880s, Kansas prairie grasses had been transformed into seas of green and golden grain. By 1900, Kansas was the nation's leading wheat-producing state, earning it the nickname the Wheat State. Kansas farmers found that the wheat bonanza was not without problems. When they had a great wheat crop, there was too much wheat on the market, forcing the price down. For example, during World War I, which lasted from 1914 to 1918, demand for wheat skyrocketed in Europe and America, and Kansas farmers earned high profits. But, soon after the war, there was too much wheat on the market, and prices fell to disastrous levels. Thousands of families were ruined. This pattern of high prices followed by decline continued into the twenty-first century.

Kansas was more than just wheat farms by the late 1800s and early 1900s. The city of Salina was one of the top flour-milling centers. Across the state, farmers made a profit with broomcorn. Parts of the plant were used to make brooms and brushes, while the seeds made excellent food for cattle and other livestock. Oil industries developed in places such as El Dorado in south-central Kansas. Salt mining became an important industry in Hutchinson. Kansas was a center for not just agricultural but also other types of economic growth.

The Depression and the Dust Bowl

The stock market crashed in 1929, and the United States entered a decade of unemployment and poverty called the Great Depression. Factory and office workers were out of work. Farm prices were so low that some farmers plowed the crops back into the ground because it was too expensive to ship them to markets. People across the country left their homes in search of jobs.

In addition to the bad economy, the Great Plains states were hit with a severe drought in the 1930s. The drought—combined with too-intensive farming and the cutting down of too many trees in order to plant more crops—turned the once-rich soil into dust. Strong winds blew the dust into dark clouds, and the region became known as the Dust Bowl. Especially severe windstorms struck in

1934 and 1935. One storm removed an estimated 300 million tons of topsoil, sent dust clouds rolling across the eastern United States, and dropped some of this dust on ships as far away as 500 miles (800 km) out in the Atlantic Ocean.

With the help of the state and federal governments, Kansas worked hard to correct conditions that produced the Dust Bowl. Millions of trees were planted in shelterbelts to hold the soil in place and to reduce winds. Better farming methods were introduced, including rotating crops and allowing areas of prairie grasses to replace crops.

The severe dust storms of the 1930s became known as black blizzards because of the way dark clouds of dust reduced visibility.

MAKING A CORN HUSK BROOM

Broomcorn is a grain once highly prized for broom-making. Now most brooms are made from synthetic fibers, but some are still made the traditional way. Broomcorn is not always easy to find, but you can make a traditional broom using regular corn husks.

WHAT YOU NEED

Six to eight ears of uncooked corn with their husks

Large pot of warm water

Ruler

Pencil

Scissors

2 yards (1.8 m) of twine or strong string

One stick, small branch, or dowel 1 foot (30 cm) long and about $\frac{1}{2}$ inch to 1 inch (1.3 to 2.5 cm) in diameter

Strip the husks from the ears of corn. Put the ears in a plastic bag in the refrigerator, to be cooked and eaten later. Soak the husks in the pot of warm water so they will be soft and easy to work with.

Using the ruler, measure 3 inches (7.5 cm) up from the bottom of the stick and mark that point with a pencil. Next, measure 2 inches (5 cm) up from the bottom. Mark that point with the pencil.

Cut off two pieces of twine, each about 9 inches (23 cm) long. You should now have a total of three pieces of twine. Set these aside nearby to be used later.

Lay the husks out flat with the tops all facing the same direction. Divide the husks into two equal piles. Gather the first pile of husks and form wide fringes by tearing each husk into several strips about three-fourths of the length of the husk. Gather the husks in your hand, with the fringe pointing down. Arrange the husks around the 2-inch (5-cm) pencil mark on the stick. Using one of the 9-inch (23-cm) pieces of string, tightly wrap the husks against the stick and tie a tight knot.

Gather the second group of husks and tear them into thin strips of fringe. Arrange this group of husks around the stick, overlapping this group with the first layer of husks. Tightly wrap the other 9-inch-long (23-cm-long) twine around this second layer, against the 3-inch (7.5-cm) mark. Tie another knot.

Starting from the place where you made your last knot, take the long piece of twine and tightly wrap it around the husks. (The best way to start this is to spread the twine out on the floor and lay the broom handle in the middle of the twine. That way when you are done wrapping the twine, the ends will be near each other.) You should wrap the twine around and down until you reach the knot you made at the 2-inch (5-cm) mark. When you reach that point, tie a tight knot and trim off the ends of the twine.

You can trim the ends of the husks to even out your broom, and then use the broom to sweep up the scraps.

Uneven Progress

Government programs helped to relieve some of the unemployment in the nation during the Great Depression. Workers were given jobs building highways, dams, and other structures. Some government programs paid workers to go to the Pacific Northwest to clear forests. World War II, which lasted from 1939 to 1945, also helped the American economy recover from the hard times of the Depression. The war created a tremendous demand for both agricultural products and manufactured goods, including weaponry and military transportation equipment. Wichita, the state's largest city, rapidly became a leading producer of small aircraft. Other kinds of manufacturing also increased greatly during the war years and after. By the 1950s, the manufacturing industries of Kansas began producing more of the state's income than agriculture. This increased revenue from manufacturing continued into the twenty-first century.

Populations across Kansas changed as the years passed. A decline in rural populations had started in the 1920s and 1930s. It continued through the 1950s and 1960s as urban and suburban communities grew. Military bases such as Schilling Air Force Base in Salina and McConnell Air Force Base in Wichita brought more families to Kansas. (Schilling became the Salina Municipal Airport in 1965.)

During the 1950s and through the 1960s, Kansas—along with the rest of the country—experienced difficulties stemming from racial discrimination. At the time, African Americans did not enjoy the same rights as white Americans. In some areas,

Many planes used by the U.S. military in World War II were manufactured in Kansas.

Linda Brown (far left in this photo, with her parents and sister) could not attend a school close to her home while segregated schools were legal in Kansas.

facilities such as schools were racially segregated. In areas with school segregation, black children and white children had to go to separate schools. In Kansas, an 1879 law allowed cities with a population of more than 15,000 to have segregated elementary schools. School segregation became the subject of a major U.S. Supreme Court case, B*rown v. Board of Education of Topeka.* It concerned several African-American children. The Brown listed in the case's title was the father of one of them, a young girl named Linda. She was not allowed to attend the all-white public school near her home and had to ride a bus across Topeka to attend the school for African-American children. In 1954, the Supreme Court ruled against segregated schools. The Court stated that in order for all children to receive equal education, schools must be integrated. This was a major step toward equal rights for minorities. It bolstered the civil rights movement, which fought for equal treatment of African Americans and other minorities.

The 1970s and 1980s were difficult times for the state's economy. In this period, a number of young people left Kansas. They were searching for better job opportunities and a different environment. In addition, low prices for agricultural products led many farm families to sell their land. To combat these trends, the state government looked for ways to provide better job opportunities for young people within the state.

Starting in the mid-1990s, Kansas witnessed an encouraging revival in

The state's universities are centers of scientific research.

business and agriculture. The state's population grew at a faster rate. Some people who had moved out of the state twenty or thirty years earlier began coming back. Many found that they preferred the slower, friendlier life in Kansas. Others said that they returned for better schools or for the clean air and water.

Kansas Today

Population growth slowed again in the early years of the twenty-first century. For the decade between the 2000 and 2010 U.S. censuses, the state population increased by 6.1 percent. The growth rate for the entire country was 9.7 percent.

In addition, Kansas was affected by the long-lasting recession, or economic downturn, that gripped the United States beginning at the end of 2007. Unemployment in Kansas rose, although not to the extent seen in most states.

The state's educational system helps keep the economy going. Kansas has more than thirty universities and colleges, roughly twenty two-year community colleges, and several technical schools. These institutions provide an educated workforce and also draw students from other states and other parts of the world.

Important Dates

★ **10,000 BCE–1700s CE** Paleo-Indians, early Indians, and their descendants live and hunt on the land.

★ **1541** Spanish explorer Francisco de Coronado reaches present-day Kansas.

★ **1682** All the land drained by the Mississippi River, including the region that is now Kansas, is claimed for France by explorer René-Robert Cavelier, sieur de La Salle.

★ **1744** The French establish Fort de Cavagnial, the first long-lasting European settlement in the Kansas area, on the west bank of the Missouri River.

★ **1803** The United States buys from France the region that includes Kansas in a deal known as the Louisiana Purchase.

★ **1827** Colonel Henry Leavenworth establishes a U.S. military outpost to help protect the Santa Fe Trail.

★ **1830–1854** The area of present-day Kansas is part of Indian Territory.

★ **1854** The Kansas-Nebraska Act creates the Kansas Territory and opens the land to settlers.

★ **1854–1861** Violence between supporters and opponents of slavery causes the Kansas Territory to be called Bleeding Kansas.

★ **1861** The eastern part of the Kansas Territory enters the Union as the state of Kansas (the thirty-fourth state) on January 29. It is a free state—one where slavery is not allowed.

★ **1916** Clyde Cessna starts building aircraft in Wichita. Eleven years later, he forms the Cessna Aircraft Company.

★ **1934–1935** The Dust Bowl strikes western Kansas and other parts of the Great Plains.

★ **1952** Dwight D. Eisenhower, who grew up in Abilene, is elected the thirty-fourth president of the United States.

★ **1954** The U.S. Supreme Court rules in the case Brown v. Board of Education of Topeka that segregation in schools is illegal.

★ **1990** Joan Finney is elected the first woman governor of Kansas.

★ **2011** Kansas celebrates its 150th anniversary as a state.

The People

Kansas is far from crowded. With a population of fewer than 3 million people, it is one of the least populous states in the nation. The 2010 U.S. Census found that thirty-two of the fifty states have more people than Kansas. In land area, however, Kansas is one of the largest states—only twelve states cover more area.

More than half of the people live in a handful of cities in eastern Kansas. Wichita is the largest city, with more than 380,000 people. Other major cities include Overland Park, Kansas City, Topeka, Olathe, and Lawrence. There are no large cities in the western half of the state. Dodge City, with around 27,000 people, is the largest.

Although most Kansans now live in urban areas, the rural population remains a vital part of the state's economic, political, and social life. There are more than 65,000 farms in the state, visible reminders of the importance of agriculture. Many Kansans live on ranches and take part in the state's livestock industry.

Diversity

Kansas's population includes people from many backgrounds. However, about 84 percent of the population is Caucasian—or white. Caucasians living in Kansas come from a variety of places. Some are descendants of the early pioneers who came from the Ohio River valley, southern states, or East Coast communities.

Young Kansans take part in a statewide program that teaches the importance of voting.

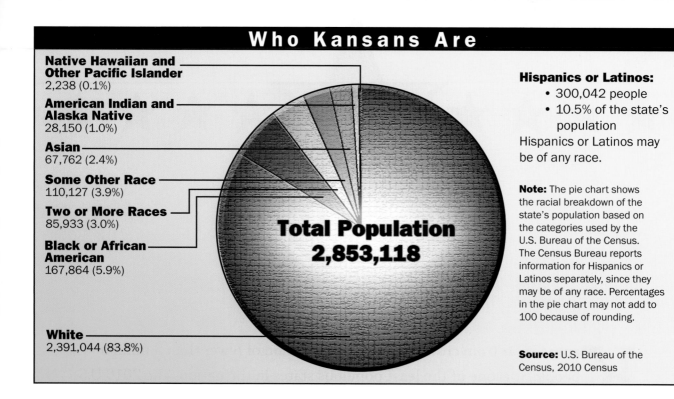

Who Kansans Are

Native Hawaiian and Other Pacific Islander
2,238 (0.1%)

American Indian and Alaska Native
28,150 (1.0%)

Asian
67,762 (2.4%)

Some Other Race
110,127 (3.9%)

Two or More Races
85,933 (3.0%)

Black or African American
167,864 (5.9%)

White
2,391,044 (83.8%)

Total Population
2,853,118

Hispanics or Latinos:
- 300,042 people
- 10.5% of the state's population

Hispanics or Latinos may be of any race.

Note: The pie chart shows the racial breakdown of the state's population based on the categories used by the U.S. Bureau of the Census. The Census Bureau reports information for Hispanics or Latinos separately, since they may be of any race. Percentages in the pie chart may not add to 100 because of rounding.

Source: U.S. Bureau of the Census, 2010 Census

Others are descended from immigrants from Europe who came to the region in the 1800s or later. Many other Caucasians in the state have come directly from other parts of the country or from other parts of the world.

People from Ireland began immigrating to Kansas in the mid-1800s, as a result of the tragedy known as the Irish Potato Famine. In the late 1840s, a disease affecting potato plants destroyed much of the potato crop in Ireland. Since potatoes were a main source of food for poor people in the countryside, the crop failure caused widespread suffering and starvation. It is estimated that perhaps one million people in Ireland died in the Irish Potato Famine. At least an equal number left Ireland in search of better lives elsewhere. Many of those immigrants came to the United States, including Kansas.

In the 1870s and 1880s, immigration from Ireland continued. In addition, immigrants from Russia and Germany came to Kansas. Many of the Russians and Germans were members of religious groups who were looking for a good place to freely practice their religions. Railroad advertising also helped draw many immigrants from the Scandinavian countries to the United States. The largest numbers of these Swedes, Norwegians, Danes, and Finns settled in more northerly states. But several thousand, mainly Swedes, settled in Kansas. The descendants of many of these homesteaders continue to live on family farms in towns such as Scandia and Lindsborg.

Today, African Americans make up almost 6 percent of the state's population. Some of these residents have moved in from other states. Others are descended from African Americans who came to the state in the 1800s as Exodusters. Many African-American Kansans are involved in politics, education, and business.

St. Patrick's Day festivities across the state honor the Irish heritage of many Kansans.

Famous Kansans

Charles Curtis: Politician and United States Vice President

Charles Curtis was born in Topeka in 1860. He was part American Indian and spent several years of his youth on a Kansa, or Kaw, reservation. Early in his career, Curtis worked as a lawyer for Shawnee County. He was a member of the U.S. House of Representatives from 1893 to 1907 and then served many years in the U.S. Senate. In 1928, he was elected vice president of the United States, with Herbert Hoover as president. He and Hoover served until 1933. Curtis died in 1936.

Dwight D. Eisenhower: Military Leader and United States President

Born in Texas in 1890, Eisenhower grew up in Abilene, Kansas, before attending the U.S. Military Academy at West Point in New York and launching a career in the U.S. Army. He rose to the rank of general and became one of the great heroes of World War II, serving as supreme commander of Allied forces in Europe. In 1952, he was elected president of the United States and served two terms as one of the most popular presidents in U.S. history. Eisenhower died in 1969.

Amelia Earhart: Aviator

Earhart was born in Atchison in 1897. In 1932, she became the first woman pilot to cross the Atlantic Ocean in a solo flight. She went on to set a number of flying records over the next five years. In 1937, with Frederick Noonan as navigator, she attempted a round-the-world flight. The plane disappeared in the Pacific Ocean, and no traces of the plane, Earhart, or Noonan were ever found.

William Inge: Playwright

William Inge was one of America's most famous playwrights. He also wrote for television and films. Born in Independence, Kansas, in 1913, he graduated from the University of Kansas. Inge is remembered as one of the first major American writers to deal with the lives of ordinary Americans in the small towns of the Midwest. His best-known plays include *Come Back, Little Sheba, Picnic,* and *Bus Stop.* He received a Pulitzer Prize for *Picnic* and an Academy Award for his screenplay for the movie *Splendor in the Grass.* Inge died in 1973.

Charlie "Bird" Parker: Jazz Musician

Charlie Parker was born in Kansas City, Kansas, in 1920. He became a famous jazz composer and saxophonist in New York City and gained the nickname "Yardbird"—or simply "Bird." With several other African-American musicians, he created a jazz style known as bebop or bop. Birdland, a New York City jazz club, was named in his honor when it opened in 1949. Parker died in 1955.

Martina McBride: Country Music Singer

Martina McBride's hits include *Independence Day, Wild Angels, Valentine*, and *Blessed.* Born Martina Mariea Schiff in Sharon in 1966, she grew up on a farm. While still a girl, she performed as a singer and keyboard player with her father's band, called the Schiffters. She married sound engineer John McBride in 1988. Her many awards include selection as the Country Music Association's Female Vocalist of the Year in 1999 and 2002–2004 and the Academy of Country Music's Top Female Vocalist in 2001–2003.

Recent Immigration

Changes in U.S. immigration laws in 1965 and 1990 led to a great increase in the numbers of legal immigrants entering the country from the Middle East, Asia, Mexico, and elsewhere in Latin America. In the 1980s, for example, more than 6 million newcomers arrived in the United States from countries in Asia and Latin America. During the same decade, fewer than one million people came from Europe, the continent of origin for the majority of Americans.

A number of Lebanese immigrants have made Kansas their home. Hailing from a country in the Middle East, these immigrants have established communities in many different Kansas cities. Several Lebanese immigrants became business leaders in Wichita and Topeka.

Today, roughly 2 percent of Kansas's population is Asian American. Some of these Kansans are immigrants from other countries, while others have families that have lived in the state for generations.

The largest minority group in the state consists of Hispanic people. People of Hispanic descent make up more than 10 percent of the state's population. Today, more than half of the population in Liberal and Dodge City is Hispanic. Many Hispanic Americans in Kansas have recently arrived in the state. Others are from families that have been longtime residents.

The museum of the Mid-America All-Indian Center in Wichita features both traditional and modern artworks and other objects created by American Indians.

Graduation day at Haskell Indian Nations University is a joyous occasion for many students.

Kansas's Indian Heritage

Before the 1800s, American Indians made up most of the region's population. Kansas's Indian heritage is unusual because so many different Indian groups have lived in the region, often at different times. Around the 1830s, the existing groups of eastern Kansas began to be joined by Indians who were moved from their land east of the Mississippi River. Although most of these Indians were later moved to Oklahoma, some remained on reservations in Kansas. Today there are reservations for the Potawatomi, Kickapoo, Sac and Fox, and Iowa tribes.

In the period when Indians from the east were being relocated to Kansas, church missionaries came to Kansas in an effort to help the various groups. One result of the missionary activity was the opening of the first school in Kansas. It was for Indian children. Later, in 1884, the United States Indian Industrial Training School was opened in Lawrence for students from different American Indian groups. It was renamed the Haskell Institute in 1887 and became Haskell Junior College in 1970. The school later expanded into today's Haskell Indian Nations University. Its students come from around the country and include members of Alaska Native groups as well as American Indian groups. It also houses the American Indian Athletic Hall of Fame.

The state's population is only about 1 percent American Indian. But Indians in the state continue to celebrate their history and culture. Festivals, powwows, and other celebrations are held throughout the year. At these gatherings people can enjoy ceremonial dances and traditional food, clothing, and crafts.

All of the different peoples and cultures of Kansas come together to make it a unique and interesting state.

Calendar of Events

★ Kansas Day

This statewide celebration is held every year on January 29. It marks the admission of Kansas as the thirty-fourth state in 1861.

★ Kansas Relays

Held at the University of Kansas in Lawrence every April, this track-and-field meet is one of the nation's classic sports events.

★ Wichita River Festival

This annual celebration takes place each year in May or June in Wichita and lasts several days. It features a variety of activities. Concerts, sports tournaments, fireworks, and a parade are just some of the highlights of this event.

★ Flint Hills Rodeo

Kansas has a number of well-known rodeos throughout the year, and the Flint Hills Rodeo at Strong City is considered one of the best. It is also the state's oldest regularly held rodeo. Every June it draws leading rodeo performers from around the country.

★ Wah-Shun-Gah Days

In June, a festival called Wah-Shun-Gah (or Washunga) Days brings together many Indians and non-Indians. The celebration is held at Council Grove, once an outpost on the Santa Fe Trail, and honors the Kansa, or Kaw, people who once lived in the area. The gathering features an intertribal powwow, a parade, dances, foods, and crafts.

★ Dodge City Days

Period costumes and activities recall the times when Dodge City was called the Cowboy Capital of the World. Front Street has been re-created, giving visitors a feeling for Wild West days. A visit to the original Boot Hill is also a must during this popular tourist event, which is held in late July or early August every year.

★ Kansas State Fair

Many counties hold fairs and rodeos in late summer, but the biggest event is the famous Kansas State Fair. It is held in Hutchinson in September. The fair highlights prize cattle and other livestock, outstanding crop yields, crafts, and cooking. It also features amusement-park rides and competitions ranging from arm wrestling and auctioneering to a debating contest and a spelling bee. Other forms of entertainment include concerts and marching bands.

★ Cider Days Fall Festival

Held annually in late September in Topeka, the Cider Days Fall Festival offers hundreds of arts and crafts booths along with rides, gunfight reenactments, food, and music performances. Not to be missed is the freshly made, natural cider.

★ Svensk Hyllningsfest

The town of Lindsborg is known as "Little Sweden," and every other October it hosts the Svensk Hyllningsfest ("Swedish Tribute Fest"), which offers a chance to experience the state's Scandinavian heritage. People dress in traditional clothing, and there are craft and food displays, along with folk music and dancing.

4

How the Government Works

Local government is important to Kansans. In the western half of the state, where towns are widely scattered, the county governments play an important role in providing services to residents of small communities and isolated farms.

In each county in Kansas, voters elect at least three commissioners, as well as other officials. These officials usually include a county clerk, a county attorney, a treasurer, a register of deeds, and a sheriff. Most cities have an elected mayor and a council. The local governments manage most of the day-to-day affairs of each community, while the state government addresses matters that are of statewide importance.

Some Kansans feel that the state government is lopsided in favor of the cities. Since all of the largest cities are in the east, the farmers and ranchers of western Kansas often feel left out, both as westerners and as rural residents. Government leaders have been trying to reduce this east-west, urban-rural tension by improving the involvement of western counties in state agencies. The Department of Health and

Quick Facts

FEWER COUNTIES?
Because of the decreasing population in parts of western Kansas, some lawmakers have suggested consolidating—or combining—smaller counties.

Built between 1866 and 1903, the Kansas State Capitol is where the state legislature meets and the governor works.

Environment, for example, brings health and nutrition information directly to the western communities and helps them to deal with matters such as food safety, water quality, and waste management.

State Government

The Kansas state government has three branches: executive, legislative, and judicial. Each branch plays a different role. The executive branch enforces the state's laws. The legislative branch—the state legislature—passes the laws. The judicial branch—the state's courts—interprets the laws and settles disputes.

The executive branch is headed by the governor, who is the state's chief executive, much as the president is the chief executive for the United States. The governor is elected to a four-year term. Other high-ranking members of the executive branch elected to four-year terms include the lieutenant governor, secretary of state, and attorney general. The governor and lieutenant governor are subject to term limits. A person cannot serve in either post for more than two terms in a row.

Voters also elect legislators, or members of the state legislature. The legislature is divided into two houses, or chambers. One chamber, the senate, is made up of forty senators, elected for four-year terms. The second chamber, the house of representatives, is made up of 125 representatives elected for two-year terms. Legislators are not subject to any term limits. The governor and the state legislature work together to handle issues that involve the whole state—for example, proposing and making new state laws and preparing and approving a budget for managing the state's affairs.

The supreme court serves as Kansas's highest court and also manages the judicial branch. It is composed of seven justices, or judges. Each justice is selected by the governor but, after one year in office, is subject to a vote by the people. If the justice wins the approval of a majority in this retention vote, he or she can serve for a six-year term, at the end of which another retention vote is held, if the justice wishes to continue serving. Kansas also has a court of appeals with thirteen judges. They, too, are chosen by the governor and are subject to

Branches of Government

EXECUTIVE ★ ★ ★ ★ ★ ★ ★ ★

The governor is the chief executive officer of the state. Other elected officials in the executive branch include the lieutenant governor, attorney general, and secretary of state. The governor appoints a number of executive branch officers, usually with the approval of the senate. In addition to seeing that the state's laws are carried out, the governor approves (signs) or disapproves (vetoes) new bills that have been passed by the legislature.

LEGISLATIVE ★ ★ ★ ★ ★ ★ ★ ★

The legislative branch is responsible for creating new laws. The legislature is made up of two houses: the house of representatives and the senate. A legislative coordinating council, consisting of a few members from each house, oversees legislative services. When the legislature is not in session, the council represents that body and governs the work of legislative committees.

JUDICIAL ★ ★ ★ ★ ★ ★ ★ ★

The judicial branch includes the state's courts. Most civil and criminal trials are held in the district courts. In jury trials, the judge makes sure proper court procedures are followed, and the jury decides the case on the basis of the evidence. If either the defense or the prosecution is not satisfied with a district court ruling, it can appeal the ruling to the state court of appeals or the Kansas supreme court. In addition to hearing appeals, the supreme court oversees the judicial branch.

a retention vote. Their term of office, however, lasts only four years. Kansas is divided into thirty-one judicial districts, each with a court that handles trials. District judges serve four-year terms. In some districts, they are chosen by election. In others they are appointed, subject to a retention election. A number of cities have a municipal court, usually dealing with minor offenses.

How a Bill Becomes a Law

Any senator or representative can propose a new law to take action on an issue that he or she feels needs the state's attention. These issues may include

The state senate meets in this room in the Capitol when the legislature is in session.

such matters as creating new parks, improving highways, or establishing agencies to care for residents. Often, ideas for new proposed laws come from citizens. A proposed law is called a bill.

Once a legislator introduces a bill in one of the houses of the legislature, it is sent to a committee consisting of several members of that house. The committee studies the bill and decides whether to recommend that the entire house consider it. The committee may hold public hearings on the bill and may change, or amend, it. If the bill makes it out of the committee, the house then decides whether to approve it, perhaps with new amendments. If a majority of the house's members vote to approve the bill, it goes to the other house.

In the second house, the bill goes through the same process as in the first. If the second house passes it without making any changes, it goes straight to the governor for his or her approval. If amendments are made in the second house, however, the modified bill goes back to the first house, which will vote on whether it accepts the bill in its new form. If the first house gives its approval, the bill then is sent to the governor. If the first house refuses to agree to the changes, however, then it can request that a "conference committee," consisting of a few members from each house, discuss the bill. The conference committee may suggest further changes to the bill to make it acceptable to both houses. If the new version of the bill gains the approval of both houses, it can then be sent to the governor.

The governor has ten days to act on the bill. If the governor signs it, it becomes law. The governor may choose to reject, or veto, the bill. In that case it goes back to the state legislature. If two-thirds of the members of each house vote in favor of it, it becomes law despite the veto. If the governor neither signs nor vetoes the bill within the allotted ten days, it automatically becomes law.

In 1933, Kansas established a way of making the legislature operate more smoothly. Legislators found that they were being overwhelmed by the number of bills being introduced. Some of these bills duplicated or contradicted other bills and laws. To overcome these problems, the legislature created an agency called the legislative council. This agency was reorganized in 1971 as the legislative coordinating council. It is made up of leading members of both houses—three from the senate and four from the house of representatives. When the house

Contacting Lawmakers

★ ★ ★ ★ ★ ★ ★ ★ ★ ★ ★ ★ ★

To get in touch with Kansas legislators you will need to find their contact information.

Go to the website

http://www.kslegislature.org/li

By following the links on the site, you can find the name and contact information of the state senator and state representative for every locality in Kansas. The site can also show you who represents the locality on the state board of education and in the U.S. House of Representatives. You can ask a parent, teacher, or librarian to help you determine which district you live in.

Quick Facts

DIFFERENT CAPITALS
Between 1854 and 1861, the Territory of Kansas had different capitals, depending, among other things, on whether supporters or opponents of slavery were in control of the state. Fort Leavenworth was the territory's first capital. Other towns that served as the capital were Shawnee Mission, Pawnee, Lecompton, Minneola, and Lawrence. In 1861, Topeka became the state capital.

and senate are not in session, the council oversees the preparation of bills for the full house and senate to consider. Its role in studying and researching the measures streamlines the lawmaking process. Several other states have used this idea in their governments.

Political Pioneers

Kansas has been one of the nation's pioneers in political matters for more than a century. When it became a state in 1861, for example, its constitution extended to women rights that they lacked in other states. The constitution granted women the right to own property, to take part in school district elections, and to have legal custody of children. In 1887, Kansas took another progressive step when women were granted suffrage, or the right to vote, in local elections. That same year, Susanna Salter was elected mayor of the town of Argonia. She was the first woman mayor of any American community. Through an amendment to the state constitution, Kansas extended voting rights to women in all elections in 1912. This was eight years before the Nineteenth Amendment to the U.S. Constitution enabled women in all states to vote.

The state also played a major role in a movement in the late 1890s that led to the creation of a political group called the Populist, or People's, Party. The Populists elected several members of Congress from Kansas in the 1890s, as well as a governor (Lorenzo Dow Lewelling) and state legislators. By the end of the decade, the party's strength faded, but Populists had the satisfaction of seeing some of their programs become law over the next twenty years. Kansas activists

A graduate of Kansas State Agricultural College, Susanna Salter was just 27 years old when she was elected mayor of Argonia.

KANSANS IN CONGRESS

Kansas is represented in the U.S. Congress in Washington, D.C. Like all states, it has two members in the U.S. Senate. The number of members each state has in the U.S. House of Representatives is related to the state's population and can change after each U.S. census is taken. Based on results of the 2010 Census, Kansas is entitled to four representatives in the U.S. House, the same number as under the previous census.

"Sockless Jerry" Simpson and Mary Lease, the "Kansas Pythoness," were two of the most fiery and famous Populist leaders. They helped to make the Populists, for a few years, one of the most successful third parties in U.S. history. (Political parties other than the two major parties are often called third parties.) Simpson served in the U.S. House of Representatives in 1891–1895 and 1897–1899.

Everyone Can Take Part

The division of Kansas into so many counties and cities enables a great number of people to be involved in local government. In addition, special councils for such groups as the elderly or the disabled have been established to advise government officials at the local and state levels.

Kansas residents of all ages are also encouraged to express their views to their local and state legislators. These officials are there to serve Kansas, and they are interested in the opinions of the people they represent.

In Their Own Words

Argonia is a pretty little city . . . with a population of 500 . . . incorporated two years ago. . . . It has attracted the attention of suffragists by electing, this spring, a lady to the mayoralty. This is the first time a woman has held that office in Kansas, and we are glad that the "innovation" is made in the person of one who will fill that office with credit to herself . . . and satisfaction to her townspeople.

—Laura M. Johns, president of the Kansas Equal Suffrage Association, writing in a Salina newspaper on April 28, 1887

Making a Living

Visitors to Kansas are often struck by how much of the state is devoted to farming and cattle grazing. In fact, about 90 percent of the land area is taken up by cropland, pasture, and cattle feedlots.

Agriculture has always been central to Kansas, but other segments of the economy have grown steadily over the past century. Today, manufacturing and service fields such as retail sales (stores), tourism, and government all play an important part in the life of the state. Each of these fields employs far more Kansans than the state's agricultural industry.

Farming

From the 1850s to the early 1900s, Kansas was almost completely an agricultural state. The pioneer farmers of that period faced enormous hardships. The warfare with American Indians ended by the late 1870s, but farm families still had to battle the thick prairie sod, periods of no rain or too much rain, and pests such as grasshoppers and rabbits. Hordes of grasshoppers could wipe out a whole season's crops in a single day.

The introduction of winter wheat helped to ease some of these difficulties. By the end of the 1800s, Kansas had become the nation's leading producer of wheat. Today Kansas is still a top wheat producer. Some of the state's wheat is exported

Farms and ranches employ far fewer Kansans today than in past decades, but they remain important to the state's economy.

to other countries, and the rest is shipped across the United States. According to the U.S. Department of Agriculture, Kansas accounts for more than 15 percent of all of the wheat grown in the United States.

Kansas farms grow more than just wheat. Wheat is the state's number one crop in terms of number of acres planted, but corn is the leading crop in terms of bushels produced and dollar value. Other important crops include sorghum, soybeans, and alfalfa. In 2009, Kansas ranked second in the nation in production of wheat and sorghum grain, third in sunflower production, fourth in summer potatoes, and fifth in hay.

A large amount of the state's agricultural production provides raw materials for businesses within Kansas. For example, much of the wheat crop goes to mills within the state where it is ground into flour. The flour is then shipped to other parts of the country and the world. Of all the states, Kansas is number one in flour milling.

Ranches across Kansas raise livestock. Cattle are the most numerous livestock, but many Kansans raise sheep, goats, chickens, and pigs. The livestock is often sent to other states. But Kansas has had its own successful meat-packing plants since the middle of the nineteenth century. A large amount of the country's beef comes from Kansas ranches.

About 4 million acres (1.6 million ha) of farmland in Kansas are devoted to growing soybeans.

RECIPE FOR WHOLE-WHEAT PANCAKES

Wheat flour is ideal for making bread, pastries, and pancakes. By following these instructions, you can make your own batch of delicious whole-wheat pancakes.

WHAT YOU NEED

$1\frac{1}{2}$ cups (200 grams) whole-wheat flour

$\frac{1}{4}$ teaspoon (1.15 g) baking soda

$1\frac{1}{2}$ teaspoons (7 g) baking powder

$\frac{1}{4}$ teaspoon (1.5 g) salt

1 tablespoon (14 g) brown sugar (packed)

1 egg

$1\frac{1}{2}$ cups (370 g) buttermilk (you can use regular milk if you cannot find buttermilk)

1 tablespoon (14 g) oil

Place the flour, baking soda, baking powder, and salt in a large mixing bowl. Mix these dry ingredients well. In a smaller bowl, combine the brown sugar, egg, buttermilk, and oil.

Pour the liquid mixture into the large bowl and mix everything together. The batter will be a little bit lumpy, but make sure that everything is moistened.

Have an adult help you with the stove. Lightly grease or butter a griddle or frying pan. Pour about $\frac{1}{4}$ cup of batter for each pancake. When bubbles appear on the surface of the pancake, carefully flip the pancake over and allow the other side to cook. Your pancakes should be a golden brown color.

You can eat your pancakes with maple syrup, fruit syrup, or a mixture of fresh fruit. You can even add chopped walnuts, blueberries, apple pieces, or chocolate chips to the batter to give your pancakes extra flavor.

Natural Resources

In addition to having some of the most fertile soil found anywhere in the world, Kansas is blessed with abundant natural resources. Oil was first discovered in the state in the 1860s, and natural gas in the 1870s. By the beginning of the 1900s the state was one of the nation's leading energy producers. Oil output began to decline after 1950, but the state continues to produce oil, as well as natural gas. In 2008, Kansas ranked ninth in the United States in oil production and tenth in natural gas production.

Mining has provided jobs for many Kansans over the years. Coal mining began in eastern Kansas in the 1850s, and for many years that part of the state was a major coal producer. Output reached nearly 6.86 million short tons (6.2 million metric tons) in 1914. Much of the coal was obtained by strip-mining: the surface soil was removed to get to the coal just below the ground. In Cherokee County, one of the largest power shovels in the world was built in 1962 for this purpose. Called Big Brutus, it can now be seen at a coal museum near West Mineral. The American Society of Mechanical Engineers has named it a regional historic mechanical engineering landmark. Strip-mining was profitable, but it also scarred the land. Nature stepped in to help the state by filling in many of the mined areas with rainwater and snow runoff, creating dozens of beautiful lakes. Today Kansas produces only a small amount of coal each year.

The Big Brutus coal shovel is sixteen stories tall and weighs 11 million pounds (5 million kilograms).

Among nonfuel substances obtained from the ground in Kansas, the one with the highest monetary value in recent years has been helium. Other notable minerals produced include cement, stone, clay, salt, and sand and gravel. For about a hundred years, beginning around 1870, Kansas was an important producer of zinc and lead.

Kansas has ample supplies of electricity. Most comes from coal-fueled generators. More than one-sixth of the electricity produced comes from the Wolf Creek nuclear power plant at Burlington. Other sources include gas-fueled generators and wind power. Deriving usable energy from Kansas's winds is a hot topic discussed across the state. In some areas, you may see row after row of wind turbines. These turbines look like sleek and modern windmills. They harness the state's strong winds and turn wind power into electricity. Kansas, however, produces nowhere near as much electricity from wind power as it could. With its wide-open, windy spaces where few people live, it could potentially use wind power to generate nearly as much electricity as the total generated in the United States in 2009 from all sources. One

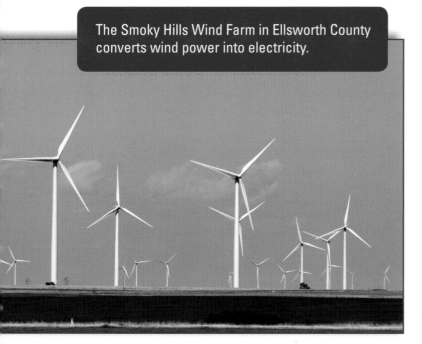
The Smoky Hills Wind Farm in Ellsworth County converts wind power into electricity.

Workers & Industries

Industry	Number of People Working in That Industry	Percentage of All Workers Who Are Working in That Industry
Education and health care	324,859	23.5%
Wholesale and retail businesses	195,870	14.2%
Manufacturing	179,565	13.0%
Publishing, media, entertainment, hotels, and restaurants	146,685	10.6%
Professionals, scientists, and managers	116,654	8.4%
Construction	91,611	6.6%
Banking and finance, insurance, and real estate	86,441	6.3%
Transportation and public utilities	64,299	4.7%
Government	63,675	4.6%
Other services	63,582	4.6%
Farming, fishing, forestry, and mining	47,295	3.4%
Totals	1,380,536	100%

Notes: Figures above do not include people in the armed forces. "Professionals" includes people such as doctors and lawyers. Percentages may not add to 100 because of rounding.

Source: U.S. Bureau of the Census, 2009 estimates

problem, however, is that special transmission lines need to be built to carry electricity from the wind turbines to other parts of Kansas. Installing these lines is costly and time consuming.

Manufacturing

Manufacturing did not become a major part of the economy until around the mid-1900s. World War I and World War II created a huge demand for manufactured goods, as well as for foods. In both wars, the United States needed weaponry, vehicles, and millions of tons of equipment, such as shoes, clothing, blankets, and bedding. Wichita, the state's largest city, became a major producer of civilian and military aircraft and gained the nickname Air Capital of the World. Today it remains an important center for aircraft manufacturing, particularly of general aviation aircraft—that is, airplanes other than those used by the military or for passenger or cargo flights. Kansas produces roughly half of the world's general aviation aircraft.

By the early 1950s, the industries of Kansas accounted for more of the state's income than agriculture. In addition to aircraft and aircraft parts, the output of the state's manufacturing plants includes railroad cars and locomotives, snowplows, trailers, camping equipment, automobile parts, and food products.

Military Bases

Several military establishments also add to the state's economy. Fort Leavenworth, for instance, became a base for military training long after its role of protecting wagon trains in the mid-1800s. The fort was used for infantry training in both World Wars. Fort Leavenworth's Command and General Staff College provides advanced training for military officers from many countries.

Fort Riley, near Junction City, also has a distinguished history. Today it is the headquarters for the U.S. Army's famous First Infantry Division, nicknamed The Big Red One. In addition, McConnell Air Force Base, at Wichita, is a center for refueling and airlift operations. Thousands of military personnel and their families add to the economy, and the bases themselves bring income to the state.

Products & Resources

Sorghum

The sorghum plant looks something like corn, and in the United States it is used primarily in feed for cattle and poultry. The grain, the stalks, and the leaves are all used to make products. The juice of one kind of sorghum is used to make a syrup, sometimes called molasses (although it is different from ordinary molasses, which is made from sugarcane or sugar beets). Sorghum is the third-largest grain crop in Kansas.

Lakes

Kansas has some natural lakes, but most of its more than 200 lakes are artificial. The largest were created by building dams on rivers or streams, and a number of lakes were created when old coal mines became filled with water. Some lakes provide drinking water for people and irrigation for crops. Some lakes also help to control flooding. Most of the lakes are also used for recreational activities such as fishing, boating, and swimming.

Wild West Towns

Abilene, Dodge City, and Wichita were some of the most famous of the old Wild West towns. These towns draw thousands of tourists every year to glimpse what life was like in the days of cowboys and long cattle drives.

Cattle

The prairie grasses that once provided feed for millions of bison now provide grazing for the state's 6 million cattle. It was in the 1870s that ranchers first discovered that cattle thrived on the short buffalo grass in the western part of the state. Since then, Kansas ranches have bred and herded cattle for food and profit.

Salt

One of the largest salt deposits in the world was formed roughly 300 million years ago when a sea covered the region that now includes Kansas. As the sea dried up, the salt was left behind, creating a huge underground deposit that covers some 27,000 square miles (70,000 sq km) in central and south-central Kansas. Near Hutchinson, where the Kansas Underground Salt Museum is located, the salt layer is more than 300 feet (90 m) thick. More than 2 million tons of salt are mined in Kansas each year.

Aircraft

The city of Wichita leads the nation in the manufacture of small civilian aircraft. In the early 1900s, aviators found that the general flatness of the land around Wichita was good for testing aircraft takeoffs and landings. Pioneering aircraft builders such as Clyde Cessna set up shop there. Today, there are more than 350 small airfields scattered throughout the state.

Service Industries

In recent years, service industries have grown markedly. Wholesale and retail trade—including supermarkets, department stores, restaurants, and gas stations—now employ more than 14 percent of all workers. Other kinds of services, such as hospitals, hotels, computer companies, and government, employ even more of the workforce. Education is also part of the service sector, and many people work in Kansas's schools, colleges, and universities. Overall, more than half of all the workers in the state are employed in some part of the service sector.

Tourism

Tourism is an important service industry. Many people come to Kansas throughout the year. Some come to see the farmland or to enjoy the lakes and parks. Kansas has more than two dozen state parks, hundreds of fishing lakes, and almost a hundred state wildlife areas. There also are several federal wildlife areas.

Sports fans visit Kansas for many athletic games. The University of Kansas Jayhawks have often contended for the national collegiate championship in men's basketball, and they have also done well over the years in women's basketball. The Jayhawk football teams have featured stars such as the legendary running back Gale Sayers. The Jayhawks' fierce rivals in the state, the Kansas State University Wildcats, have enjoyed successful years in football and both men's and women's basketball as well. The state's best-known professional sports team is soccer's Sporting Kansas City. Under its former name, Kansas City Wizards, it won the Major League Soccer championship in 2000. In June 2011, the team opened a new state-of-the-art soccer stadium, billed as the first authentic soccer stadium in the United States. Motor-racing fans flock to the Kansas Speedway in Kansas City and to Heartland Park Topeka.

Other visitors come to experience the history that the state offers. Tourists can visit Kansas's natural history at Monument Rocks or in fossil beds in western Kansas. Human history is displayed in the historic towns, museums, and sites across the state. These include a number of national historic trails and sites. Segments of the California, the Lewis and Clark, the Oregon, the Pony Express, and the Santa Fe national historic trails are in Kansas. In addition to Nicodemus, national historic sites located in Kansas include the *Brown v. Board of Education* site in Topeka, Fort Larned near the town of Larned, and Fort Scott in Bourbon County. Among the more popular museums in the state are the Eisenhower Presidential Library and Museum at Abilene, the Kansas Aviation Museum at Wichita, the Kansas Museum of History in Topeka, and the Mid-America Air Museum at Liberal.

Whatever their reasons for visiting, tourists stay at hotels, eat at restaurants, and shop in the stores. All of this brings in money for the state and creates jobs for hard-working Kansans.

The Kansas Speedway can seat more than 72,000 auto racing fans.

Areas of Growth

Sailing and other water sports may not be the first thing that comes to mind when people think of Kansas. But in recent decades, interest in sailboating and sailboat races has risen. The more than forty state-managed lakes and the many state parks draw large numbers of vacationers and tourists every year. The state also offers excellent facilities for fishing, camping, and hiking.

Computer-related businesses have also grown in recent years, especially in publishing and space exploration. Several Kansas industries are involved in the manufacture and testing of satellites and other space-related hardware. In addition, the Kansas Cosmosphere and Space Center in Hutchinson, affiliated with the Smithsonian Institution in Washington, D.C., draws thousands of visitors every year to view the largest collection of space artifacts outside of the Smithsonian's National Air and Space Museum.

Balancing Work and the Environment

Kansas has managed to avoid some of the serious environmental problems that have troubled more heavily urban states. The worst forms of air pollution and water pollution have not developed in Kansas, but there are still serious environmental concerns. The use of chemical fertilizers, for example, and the expansion of cattle feedlots produce pollutants that spread into streams and lakes, causing health hazards. One approach to such problems in Kansas was the creation of the Department of Health and Environment. The agency has considerable authority to halt activities that may be harming the environment or human health. The matter is then reviewed for whatever corrective action is needed.

State Flag & Seal

The state flag was adopted in 1927. The state seal is in the center on a blue field. It lies below the state crest, which consists of a sunflower (the state flower) above a twisted blue-and-gold bar that stands for the Louisiana Purchase. The word Kansas was added to the flag in 1961.

The seal, adopted in 1861, includes the rising sun, which stands for the East, where the pioneer settlers came from. The scene shows a farmer plowing in front of a pioneer cabin. Behind the farmer are covered wagons heading west. In the background are American Indians hunting bison. The river and steamboat represent commerce. There are thirty-four stars in the cluster at the top—indicating that Kansas is the thirty-fourth state. The Latin phrase above the stars, "Ad astra per aspera" ("To the stars through difficulties"), is the state motto. The date at the bottom, "January 29, 1861," is when Kansas joined the Union.

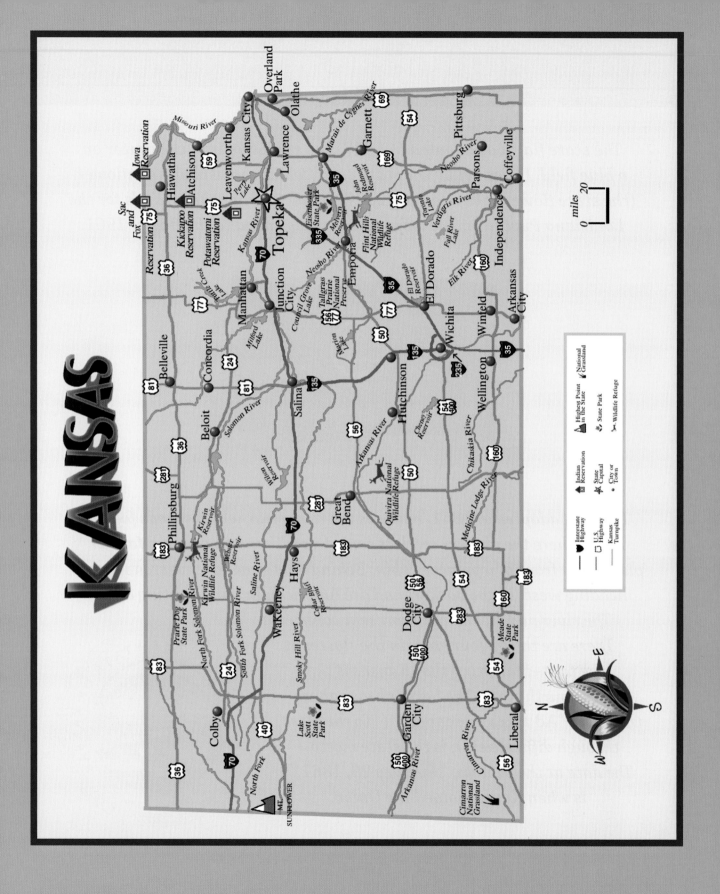

KANSAS

Overland Park
Olathe
Kansas City
Lawrence
Leavenworth
Hiawatha
Atchison
59
Missouri River
Iowa Reservation
Sac and Fox Reservation
75
Kickapoo Reservation
Potawatomi Reservation
75
Perry Lake
Topeka
335
Eisenhower State Park
Meyern Reservation
Marais de Cygnes River
Garnett
69
54
Pittsburg
169
Neosho River
75
John Redmond Reservoir
Toronto Lake
Verdigris River
Parsons
Coffeyville
Independence
Kansas River
70
Neosho River
Flint Hills National Wildlife Refuge
Fall River Lake
Elk River
160
Arkansas City
Winfield
El Dorado
35
El Dorado Reservoir
Emporia
Tallgrass Prairie National Preserve
Council Grove Lake
Junction City
Manhattan
77
Tuttle Creek Lake
Milford Lake
56
77
Marion Lake
Neosho River
77
Wichita
135
50
235
35
Wellington
Chikaskia River
160
Belleville
81
Concordia
24
81
Beloit
36
281
Phillipsburg
183
Solomon River
Wilson Reservoir
Salina
135
56
281
Great Bend
Arkansas River
Quivira National Wildlife Refuge
Cheney Reservoir
Hutchinson
54
400
50
Medicine Lodge River
160
183
Kirwin National Wildlife Refuge
Kirwin Reservoir
Webster Reservoir
North Fork Solomon River
South Fork Solomon River
Saline River
Cedar Bluff Reservoir
Prairie Dog State Park
Smoky Hill River
Hays
WaKeeney
70
183
50
56
Dodge City
283
54
160
183
Meade State Park
54
Colby
40
70
36
Lake Scott State Park
83
24
North Fork
Garden City
50
400
Arkansas River
Cimarron River
83
Liberal
56
Cimarron National Grassland
MT. SUNFLOWER
North Fork

miles
0   20

N
E
S
W

LEGEND
Interstate Highway
U.S. Highway
Kansas Turnpike
Indian Reservation
State Capital
City or Town
National Grassland
Highest Point in the State
State Park
Wildlife Refuge

State Song

Home on the Range

words by Brewster Higley
music by Daniel Kelly

BOOKS

Blair, Mike. *A Kansas Year*. Lawrence, KS: University Press of Kansas, 2009.

Fleming, Candace. *Amelia Lost: The Life and Disappearance of Amelia Earhart*. New York: Schwartz & Wade, 2011.

Gray, Lisa Waterman. *Kansas: An Explorer's Guide*. Woodstock, VT: Countryman Press, 2011.

Knopf, David. *Historic Photos of Kansas*. Nashville, TN: Turner, 2010.

WEBSITES

Kansas.gov—The Official Web Site of the State of Kansas:
www.kansas.gov

Kansas Historical Society:
www.kshs.org

Kansas Travel and Tourism:
www.travelks.com

David C. King is an award-winning author who has written more than forty books for children and young adults. He and his wife, Sharon, live in the Berkshires at the junction of New York, Massachusetts, and Connecticut. Their travels have taken them through most of the United States.

Richard Hantula is a writer and editor who lives in New York City.

Page numbers in **boldface** are illustrations.